Salmon River

Salmon River

Rick Kustich

Frank
Amato
PORTLAND

River Journal

Volume 3, Number 2, 1995

Rick Kustich is author of *Fly Fishing the Great Lakes Tributaries.* He is a respected fly fishing instructor, guide and seminar speaker. His articles have appeared in a number of fly fishing publications. Rick is involved in many conservation issues concerning the future of our fisheries. He fly fishes year-round for a wide variety of species and has developed a special passion for steelhead. He lives in Grand Island, New York.

◆

Acknowledgments

There are many anglers that I have shared special experiences with on the Salmon River including my brother Jerry Kustich, who also assisted in editing the text; Brian Slavinski, who in addition to aiding with much of the photography, tied the flies that appear in the fly plate; Don Kwiatowski, and Keith and Walt Myott. Many thanks to Les Wedge, Fred Kuepper, Mike Miller, Jerry Senecal, Bill Reed, Shirl Guenther, and Lou Baum. And especially to my wife, Ann, for her constant support and our many fly fishing experiences together.

◆

Series Editor: Frank Amato

Subscriptions:
Softbound: $29.90 for one year (four issues)
$55.00 for two years
Hardbound Limited Editions: $80.00 one year, $150.00 for two years
Frank Amato Publications, Inc. • P.O. Box 82112 • Portland, Oregon 97282 • (503) 653-8108

Design: Joyce Herbst
Photography: Rick Kustich (except as otherwise noted)
Map: Tony Amato
Printed in Hong Kong
Softbound ISBN: 1-57188-004-6, Hardbound ISBN: 1-57188-005-4
(Hardbound Edition Limited to 500 Copies)

SALMON RIVER

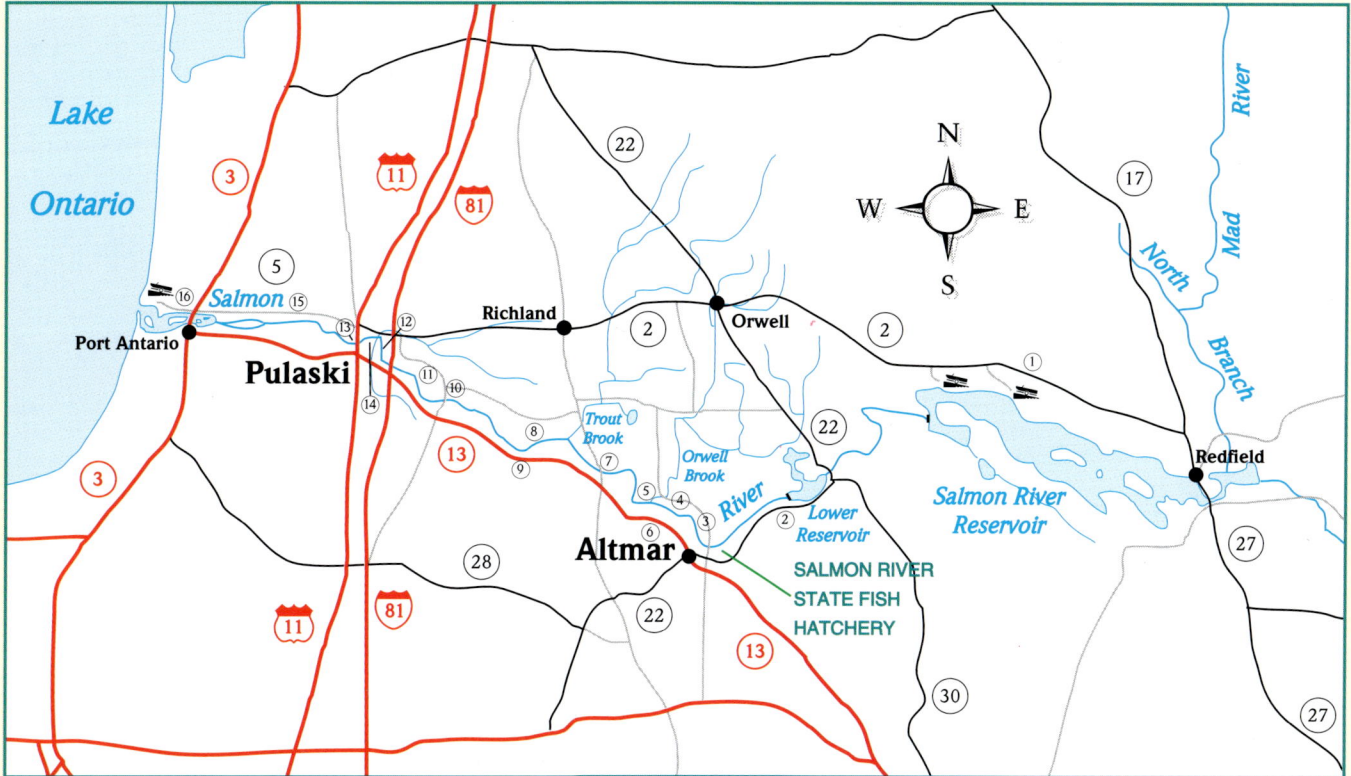

MAP CONTINUED BELOW

NEW YORK

MAPPED AREA

Salmon River Access Points

1. Little America fishing access and boat launch
2. Upper Fly Fishing Area parking lot
3. County Route 52 fishing access and boat launch
4. Ellis Cove fishing access
5. Trestle Pool - North Fishing access
6. Trestle Pool - South Fishing access
7. County Route 48 fishing access and boat launch
8. Sportsman's Pool - North fishing access
9. Sportsman's Pool - South fishing access
10. County Route 2A fishing access and boat launch
11. Railroad/papermill access
12. Parking lot behind Tony's Salmon Country Sports Shop.
13. Boat launch off Forest Drive
14. Ball Park parking lot off Dunbar Road
15. Douglaston Salmon Run parking and access lot
16. Estuary - boat launch

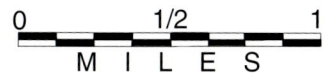

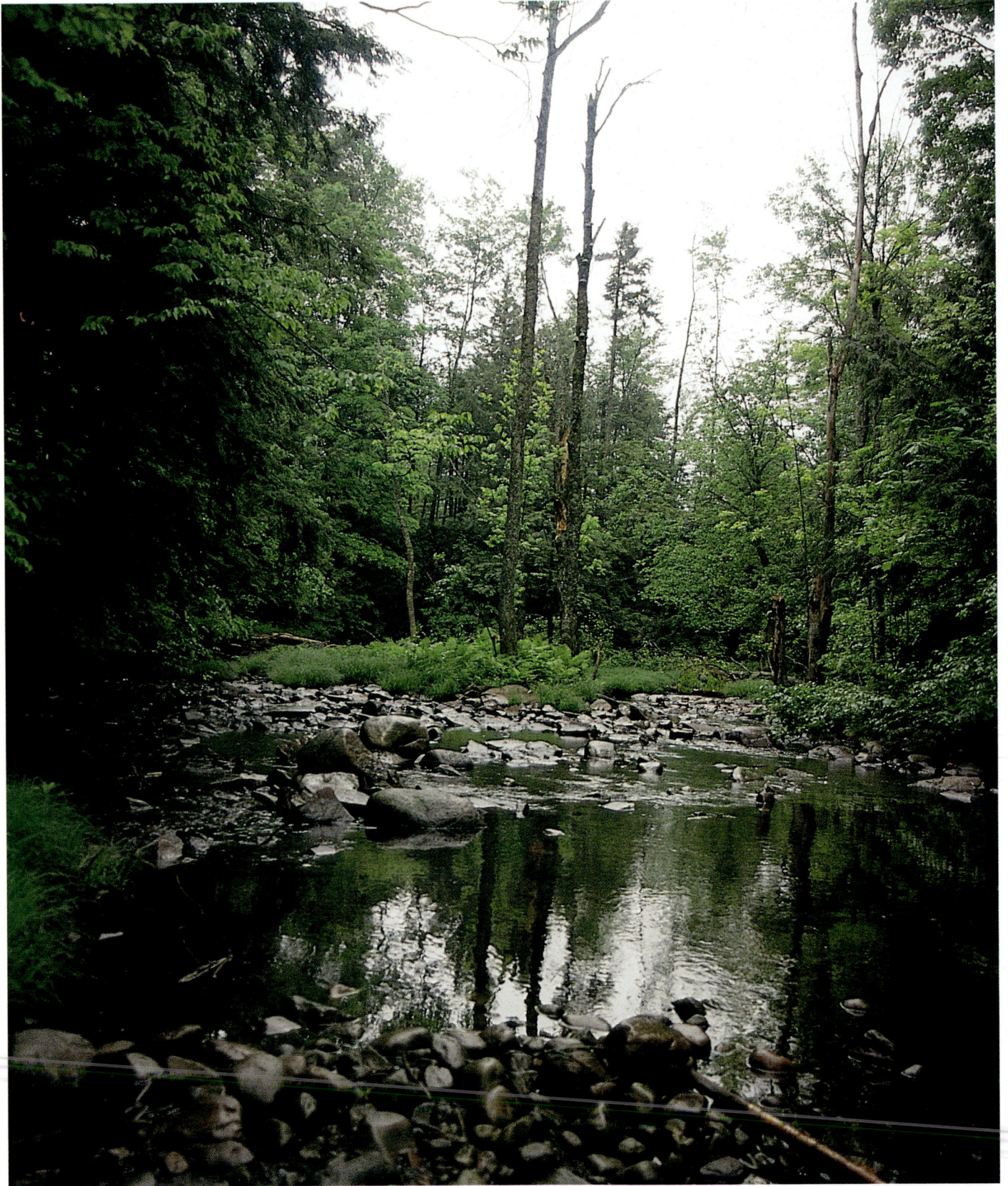

◆

Solitude on the upper river.

SALMON RIVER

◆

*T*HERE I STOOD, SPEECHLESS, AS I ATTEMPTED TO PIECE together the events that had just unfolded. I had been peaceful-ly fishing a pretty section of water. On my last cast the method-ical presentation of the fly turned violent. Suddenly, my fly line raced upstream at such a pace that the noise of it ripping through the water's surface could be heard across the pool. My reel sang out loudly and all at once there was a tremendous dis-turbance. Fifteen pounds of bright silver came catapulting out of the water. The fish fought with a fury I had never experi-enced. But, there was too much line on the water, too much tension, and in an instant the mighty fish was gone.

It recently occurred to me that some of the most memo-rable fish that I have come in contact with are not always those I actually have been able to touch. Sometimes the "one that got away" leaves an even greater imprint on one's mind. Such is the case with this large steelhead which I hooked a number of years ago on New York's Salmon River. Its sheer power was simply awesome. It was this fish that has forever hooked me on this productive river.

While one specific fish first grabbed my attention, it is diversity that may best characterize the Salmon River. Few river systems can match the fishing opportunity that exists throughout its length. This diverse nature can also be seen in its surroundings, which ranges from urban to near wilderness. The Salmon literally runs through the middle of the historic vil-lage of Pulaski. However, much of the river is relatively unspoiled and provides some of the most picturesque back-drops to be found anywhere in the Northeast.

The Salmon River has suffered from somewhat of an iden-tity crisis. Its lower 16 miles receive tremendous runs of tro-phy-size fish from Lake Ontario. But, it has become as famous for the hordes that pursue the fish, specifically the Chinook salmon, as it has for the fish itself. This reputation has left many with the feeling that a quality experience is difficult to find. In many respects this reputation has been unfairly inflat-ed. Today there is good news. Regulations and attitudes are changing. The result is increased and improved opportunity for sport fishing. One cannot help but feel that the Salmon is at the dawning of a new age.

The Salmon means many things to many people. To some it is the concentrations of big fish. To others it is the cama-raderie. Anglers can be found along the river bank sharing a few stories over a hot cup of coffee. Some seem to enjoy this as much as the fishing. To me it is a river of great challenge. It is a puzzle to be solved each day on the water and the solution is usually not constant. Finding willing fish and properly present-ing the fly is only part of the equation. To land fish on this river can be a challenge in itself, caused by powerful fish and the Salmon River's characteristic heavy flows. But the rewards are great. It is a river that only rarely allows itself to be conquered. But this is what brings me back.

The Salmon River has always attracted people. Before the time of European settlers, tribes of the Iroquois Nation used the river extensively. They camped along its banks and utilized it for fishing. They also hunted in the large mature forests that surrounded the river. In the 1700s settlers used the river to transport pelts to supply the booming fur trade.

In the early 1800s the village of Pulaski was established. Most of the trees along the river were cut and used in the settlement of the new village. Settler's were attracted to this vast waterway for a number of reasons. The most important may have been the fish. Tremendous runs of salmon. Ironically, not the Chinook salmon that the river has become noted for in recent years, but Atlantic salmon. It was the Atlantic salmon after which the river was named. They were native to Lake Ontario which was host to such a vast population that it nearly defies comprehension. One settler's account was spelled out in the *New York Fish and Game Journal,* January 1982:

"In October, 1836, two men took [on the Salmon River at Pulaski] two hundred and thirty Salmon between 8 p.m. and 12, with spears and fire-jacks, and after 12 till morning two other men in the same skiff took two hundred odd, the average weight of the entire lot being fourteen and three-quarters pounds. We have had fifteen hundred fresh Salmon in the fish-house at one time. When a freshlet occurred [sic] in June a few would always come up, and sometimes a few in the spring. Any time from June till winter when there was a fresh-let they were sure to come. The principal time, however, was in fall, during September, October, and November. Twelve skiffs in one night have taken an average of three hundred Salmon each." (George Goode, 1884:473).

With all these fish it is amazing and disheartening to learn that by 1872, the Salmon River was the only tributary to Lake Ontario where salmon were still found. By 1898, the runs of the Salmon River were also decimated and this great population was lost forever. The decline can be attributed to man's basic inability to conserve, a problem that we still face today. Over-fishing and habitat destruction are thought to be the specific causes. Mill dams prohibited the salmon from reaching preferred spawning water. Erosion resulting from deforestation combined with pollution from tanneries reduced the water quality for reproduction. In less than one hundred years the settlers had destroyed what had originally drawn them to the river.

The late 1800s were not particularly good times for the Pulaski area. Coupled with the demise of the salmon was "the great fire of 1881" which destroyed a significant portion of the village. However, it was rebuilt with some very interesting and attractive architecture. Much of this still exists today.

Except for smallmouth bass, a failed attempt to re-establish the Atlantic salmon, and limited steelhead returns, little fishing opportunity existed in the river during the early to mid 1900s. But, resiliency is a common characteristic of a truly great river. The late 1960s marked a rebirth of the Great Lakes including the Salmon River. The state of Michigan began a very successful coho and Chinook salmon stocking program in Lake Michigan with fish that were transplanted from the Pacific coast. Early efforts were aimed at controlling population explosions of exotic species such as the rainbow smelt and alewife. The stockings quickly obtained their objective while establishing a sport fishery.

The New York State Department of Environmental Conservation (DEC), along with the province of Ontario and the Fishland Wildlife Service began experimental stocking in

---

Selecting the right fly.

Lake Ontario. They were met with limited success because of another introduced species, the sea lamprey. Lamprey control began in 1971 and was continued through federal funding and involvement. Once the control began taking hold, the stockings proved to be very fruitful.

Steelhead were then stocked in the early 1970s. Some steelhead populations had existed in Lake Ontario since the late 1800s. However, it does not seem that a significant run of fish had established itself in the Salmon prior to this time. Brown trout were also added to the mix.

All the introduced species returned to the Salmon River and almost instantly a river fishery was established. There was even some natural reproduction in the tributaries to the main river. Reproduction in the river itself was limited by two hydroelectric dams built in the early 1900s. The potential of this fishery was very obvious. The key was continued lamprey control and more fish.

With this potential, the DEC developed a state-wide program to improve hatchery production. As part of the plan, the Salmon River Fish Hatchery was to be constructed. And while hatchery fish represent a poor substitute for lost native stocks, the new high technology facility would be capable of producing the levels of salmonids that would eventually make the Salmon River famous again for its runs of fish.

Construction of the hatchery, near Altmar, began in 1977 and became operational in 1981. Today the Salmon River Hatchery produces nearly five million trout and salmon annually to be stocked in New York state waters. Many are released into the Salmon River. This is an impressive operation and is a favorite point of interest to both anglers and tourists. The hatchery is open to visitors from 9 a.m. to 4 p.m. seven days a week from March 15 to November 30.

One negative aspect of the present day stocking program is that it provides the indication that the Salmon River fishery is of a strictly put and take nature. To the surprise of many, solid reproduction on Salmon River tributaries such as Orwell Brook and Trout Brook produce a large number of wild fish. It is estimated that as much as 30 to 40 percent of the annual steelhead run is comprised of naturally reproduced fish. In addition, 10 to 15 percent of the Chinook salmon and brown trout returning to the river are wild fish. Despite man's tampering, this river system remains quite fertile and it is important to respect and protect the wild stocks.

The Fishery Today

The current lower Salmon River fishery is built on the returns of salmonids from Lake Ontario. They are large fish, of trophy proportions, at least by eastern standards. To be successful, an understanding of the fish, their habits and the timing of their return is critical. The fish returning from the lake are limited to 16 miles of river up to the first power generation dam.

The Chinook or king salmon typically begins its ascent on the river in late August and intensifies throughout the first two weeks of September. These fish average 20 pounds with some

Bull thistle. Bill Reed photo.

in the 30 to 40 pound range taken each year. The Chinook has been a greatly misunderstood fish since the beginning of the current fisheries program. All Pacific salmon die naturally after they have returned to the river and spawned. The Chinook normally lives three to five years in the lake before returning. Since its main instinct is the propagation of the species, it does not feed with any regularity once in the river. This reputation quickly lead to unethical fishing practices in some areas of the river. It even prompted DEC to allow the appalling act of snagging as a legal means to take Pacific salmon. Only now is snagging in New York state on its last leg. A somewhat embarrassing situation for New York state and all sport fishing anglers.

The paradox here is that Chinooks will take a fly very well even when in the river. While their desire to feed may be limited, you must play upon their aggressive behavior. Fishing the river in its lowest three or four miles is the best approach for the early part of the run. Here fresh-run fish will eat a properly presented fly, perhaps out of impulse. Fish will normally be found resting in pockets at the head of or below heavy riffles. They will also be found in the heavier water at the heads of pools. Chinooks can be difficult and do not necessarily take on the first cast or at all. This fishing can take patience. At other times it can be simple. The early run kings are the most desirable. Sometimes they are bright fish, still in near prime shape and able to provide a fierce struggle.

This can be a pleasant time of year to fish the river. Temperatures will normally be around 70 degrees. Some days will be even hotter. It is usually the rainy days which are desired. Rain and overcast skies bring fish up from the lake and estuary. Fish on the move, that rest during their journey, seem to take a fly best.

The Chinook will also take a fly very well when near their spawning beds. Their territorial nature can make them very

A male Chinook or "king" salmon is released after a fierce battle.

◆

edgy. Protection of their space may include chomping down on a fly that comes too close. This is especially true of fish that have not been unduly harassed. Chinooks normally congregate around their spawning areas in the first two to three weeks of October. At times the fish will be visible. The foliage at this time of year can, in itself, make it worth being on the river.

Coho salmon also move into the river at nearly the same time as the Chinook, but normally a week or two later. They average six to eight pounds with some exceptions. The world record coho of 33 pounds, 4 ounces was caught in the Salmon River. Coho are much less numerous than the king. This is simply a function of the number of each species stocked in the river.

I can still remember the smell of damp leaves that lined the river, the unmistakable sign of my favorite time of year. The morning mist had given way to a steady rain. We cast our flies into the newly opened waters of the fly fishing only section above Altmar. I'm not sure if it was the lack of publicity for its opening or the deteriorating weather, but we had the river to ourselves. The bonus was that it was filled with Chinook, and as we found out, aggressive Chinook. Fish moved up the river all day long, some staying long enough to take a fly or two. We did battle with numerous fish. Timing can be everything.

The steelhead has emerged as the people's choice for favorite fish among Salmon River fly fisher's. Its fight is unparalleled in freshwater. Steelhead continue to feed while in the river and take a fly very well at times. Fishable numbers can be found in the Salmon River from September through May. Steelhead spawn in spring, but filter in during the preceding months.

Two strains of steelhead are currently stocked. Both have been obtained from the state of Washington. The most plentiful is the Chambers Creek strain. This is referred to as a winter-run fish. The peak of the run for this strain occurs in October and November. Normally, a good movement of fresh steelhead occurs during the last two weeks of October. Fresh fish filter into the river all winter, right up to spawning time. The other strain used is the Skamania. This is a summer-run fish. Under the right conditions, this strain can be found in the river during the summer months. Currently, summer water temperature and flow is not conducive to consistent runs of fish, and the angling possibilities are very limited. However, future improvements to river management through cool water summer releases may change this situation.

Steelhead that have just moved in from the lake will generally be the most aggressive toward a fly and give the best fight. Their most active temperature range is 42 to 58 degrees.

Steelhead will still take a fly after the water has fallen below 40 degrees, but it may take some coaxing. Actually a sharp decrease in temperature, even if within the optimum range, seems to slow steelhead activity until they become acclimated. Close monitoring of water temperatures is important. Fast runs and pocket water will be preferred lies in optimum temperatures. Taking a lie in slower pools becomes more common in colder water.

Salmon River steelhead average six to 12 pounds with those in the 12 to 18 pound range caught on a fairly regular basis. There are even a few legitimate 20 pounders taken on flies. The annual returns can be quite impressive. This is a result of large numbers of steelhead stocked in the river combined with natural reproduction. Annual stocking figures range around 125,000 for the Chambers Creek strain and 25,000 for the Skamania strain. In addition, 25,000 non-migratory, domestic rainbow trout are planted each year, in the lake, near the mouth of the river. Some of these fish find their way into the Salmon.

The steelhead is the fish of the future with respect to the management of tributary fishing in the Great Lakes. It is a mystical fish developing a vast following. These are people who get a certain look in their eye when the subject presents itself. They closely monitor weather and water conditions, trying to time their presence on the river with a fresh movement of fish. They fish the river during the week to beat the crowds and tolerate whatever extremes Mother Nature can dish out. For such effort they are commonly rewarded with silver torpedoes and great memories. Sometimes the only thing gained is a greater knowledge and appreciation for this great fish, but that in itself is a worthy consolation. I have become one of these people and enjoy all its aspects.

Overshadowed by the salmon and steelhead are the lake-run brown trout. As are their counterparts, these are big fish, averaging five to eight pounds. Browns from eight to 15 pounds are caught quite often. There are even a few bigger fish. The Lake Ontario tributaries, specifically the Salmon River, represent this continent's best wide-spread opportunity to catch trophy-size browns on a fly. Lake-run browns can normally be found from September through November, but not in the concentrations of salmon or steelhead. Actually, most that are caught, are done so while fishing for other species. They are handsome fish. Males generally have hooked jaws and are dressed in spawning colors that appear almost orange.

Recent attempts to re-establish Atlantic salmon into the river have been met with very limited success. A few are caught each year. There is some optimism for the future for this program. On rare occasions lake trout can be found in the lower river. Smallmouth bass are common in spring and early summer.

In the upper reaches of the river exists a link to the days of Iroquois tribes and an untouched wilderness. The brook trout is native to the Salmon River drainage and some of the original strain still exists today. In stark contrast to the lower river, the fish are small, some only five to six inches. But they are among the most beautiful creatures found on this earth. Pursuing

A fresh-run steelhead—12 pounds of pure silver.

brookies with a one or two weight fly rod can be both relaxing and productive. Some fish in the eight to ten inch range can readily be found with a few larger fish encountered on occasion. June is probably the best month. On a visit to the river this past June my wife and I were greeted by eager fish that came to our flies on every few casts.

Feisty wild rainbows also fill the upper reaches. They are usually airborne as soon as they feel the point of the hook. In the summer they become wily and selectively feed on small offerings. The origination of this wild fish is not clear, but seems to date back to the 1930s. The average size of rainbows is slightly larger than the brook trout. Brook trout and rainbows are also stocked at certain points on the river to provide a greater catch ratio for anglers.

Largemouth bass and panfish can be found in the reservoirs. Largemouths can be seen chasing their prey in the mornings and evenings. They will take a deer hair fly fished on the surface with a mighty explosion.

Unspoiled Beauty

The Salmon River begins its course in the foothills that surround the famous Adirondack Mountains. Actually, the East Branch and North Branch of the Salmon flow into the Redfield or upper reservoir to form the main river. The East and West Forks of the East Branch begin in the near wilderness of the town of Osceola, draining a portion of the Tug Hill Plateau. There is little access to the pristine upper few miles visited only by the hearty adventurer. The East Branch is fed by numerous small brooks. Most are tight, overgrown and difficult to fly fish, but some hold healthy populations of native brook trout. The biggest brookies in the area are commonly found in the small secluded pockets and holes of some of these brooks.

◆

Fiesty wild rainbows are abundant in the East Branch.

The headwaters of the North Branch flow from the remote Littlejohn Wildlife Management Area. Being fed by a few small drainages, the North Branch gains a good portion of its flow from the Mad River, which joins in approximately three miles before it enters the reservoir. The Mad in itself is a respectable piece of water.

The upper river is the softer side of the Salmon. Just within a short drive its whole complexion is reversed. The fishing here is for small stream trout and gets no major fishing pressure. Many of the classic eastern mayfly hatches emerge from these upper waters including Hendricksons, March Browns, Sulphurs and Cahills. I also found clouds of morning *Trico* spinner falls in the summer which produced difficult fishing for wary trout. There is also abundant caddis hatches.

Quite simply, this is a beautiful place. Much of the water in this upper area is lined with a thick canopy of evergreen and hardwoods. The flows are peaceful, with gentle riffles giving way to small pockets or runs. Some deep pools are formed by deadfalls or driftwood piles. The size of the water increases as it flows toward the reservoir. In the upper reaches, brook trout can be found in water only a few inches deep. Throughout their course, the North and East Branches hold trout in any water that gives the fish a little security. This includes typical trout holding water and especially along log jams and near overhanging brush.

This is easy wading water. Positioning yourself in the river and fishing upstream is commonly required to keep your fly on the water and out of the trees. There certainly does not have to be a hatch in progress to bring these fish to the surface. Fishing a dry fly in good holding water can find surprising results. May and June will see the main hatches. Although eager in spring and early summer, with the advance of summer conditions, these fish can become much more difficult to catch. Water temperatures can slow the fishing in the summer as both the East and North Branch are capable of reaching the low 70 degree range. The water quality of the East Branch appears to be better than that of the North Branch resulting in greater numbers of native and wild fish in the East Branch.

Although the East and North Branch are primarily fished by anglers within a reasonable proximity, those from afar should also consider their fertile waters. Spring steelheaders and late summer, early fall salmon fishermen would find them a pleasant change. The open season on the East and North Branches is April 1 through September 30.

New York state has secured public fishing easements on nearly 13 miles of the East Branch. Official state access points can be found where the river intersects with Waterbury Road, just above its entry into the reservoir, Ryan Road and North Osceola Road. Access to the North Branch can be found on County Route 47, Harvester Mill Road, Randall Road and Abes Road. There is approximately 11 miles of public fishing easements on the North Branch. The best opportunity for bigger fish will be found by hiking in from the main access points. Also, some larger brook trout and rainbows will be found in the slow water of the East and North Branch where it flows into the reservoir. This water is probably best accessed from a canoe.

Dry fly fishing on the East Branch.

◆

The Bennetts Bridge dam and power facility was constructed in 1913 and formed the Redfield Reservoir. It is a pretty body of water consisting of some 3,100 acres. The shores are undeveloped since a majority of the adjacent land is owned by New York state and Niagara Mohawk, the utility company which operates the power facility. There is a boat launch at the Little America Fishing access on the northwest end, off County Route 2. I have found good largemouth bass fishing in the bays and fingers of the reservoir.

The river then travels approximately three miles down to the lower reservoir. This section of the river has little angling value. However, it is host to one of the river's most scenic points, the 110 foot high Salmon River Falls. There is a parking area used for access to observe the falls along Falls Road. Water levels fluctuate widely due to power generation activities, giving the falls many different looks depending on the season. Spring run-offs normally provide the heaviest flows. These fluctuations are responsible for the poor quality of the fishing in this stretch of the river. Also, much of this section has been altered in a way that does not provide adequate holding water.

The Lighthouse Hill dam and power facility was built in 1930 and formed the 151 acre lower reservoir. In the past this facility was operated at peaking mode, which means that it generated power at times of highest demand. This created a large problem. Water levels would fluctuate greatly from day to day

or even hour to hour. Not only did this management scheme have a negative effect on the runs of fish, it created a very dangerous situation for wading the river. Thankfully such wild deviations in water flow from power generation are a thing of the past. Cooperation from Niagara Mohawk has resulted in a system of gradual changes in flow. The Lower Reservoir has largemouth bass, stocked trout and panfish.

◆

Black-eyed Susans are common in open areas near the river.

Access points are clearly marked. The new fly fishing section is the result of a team effort.

◆

The Lower River

Below the Lighthouse Hill facility is the 16 miles of water that can be accessed by fish moving upriver from Lake Ontario. These runs of salmon and trout provide a world class fishery deserving the main focus of this work. This is a river that has already been discovered by many creating at times, a crowding problem. Although some have the feeling that the typical Salmon River experience is elbow to elbow, such fishing conditions are normally restricted to the popular fishing areas at the peak of the Chinook salmon run. The quality of the experience is diminished more by the lack of respect exhibited by some anglers toward the fish, in particular the Chinook salmon, than by the numbers utilizing the resource. Unfortunately, this lack of respect is not limited merely to annual visitors of the river, but to a few guides and business owners as well.

The difficulty in forcefully patrolling the river for illegal fishing practices leaves this negative behavior unchecked. This does not imply a lack of opportunity during the salmon run. Most of the crowds are concentrated in the big name pools. Some of the lesser pools and pockets between the pools can receive low fishing pressure, yet, this water represents some of the best places to fair hook Chinook salmon.

Alternatively, there is the privately controlled Douglaston

Salmon Run. For a small fee, anglers are allowed to fish on two and a half miles of prime water. There is a limited number of anglers allowed to access this section per day. The area is patrolled and the philosophy is simple—unsportsmanlike fishing and unethical practices will not be tolerated. This section of water represents an example of management that hopefully will spread to the remainder of the river. In addition to a pleasant environment, the Douglaston Salmon Run encourages catch and release, and has put in place daily kill limits that are lower than those imposed by New York state.

Once the salmon run is over, the angling pressure is greatly reduced. Now comfortable fishing conditions can be found throughout, but not without a little effort at times. Famous pools can still see steady pressure throughout fall, but the experienced fly fishing steelheader knows that fish can be located in a variety of water, including the pockets and small runs between the pools. Fishing during the week can help avoid some of the peak angling times. Later in the season, fewer people are found on the river. I can recall a number of times within the last few years in late fall, winter and spring where I have fished the river with very few, if any, other anglers in sight.

A dramatic increase in drift boat traffic adds yet another dimension to the problems of people and pressure. For the most part, boat operators are guides who have a healthy respect for other anglers. However, an increase in negative incidents are a result of an ever-growing number of operators. This is a potential problem that may need to be addressed in the future.

Yes, there can be a lot of people. But, this is a tremendous river hosting an equally impressive fishery. With a positive attitude, confidence and a little effort, a quality experience is waiting to be discovered each and every time your on the river.

The lower river can be split into four areas. The fly fishing areas, the stretch from the Altmar Bridge to the Route 81 bridge, the section through the village of Pulaski and the Douglaston Salmon Run. Public access to the first three sections is very good. There is currently one county and eight New York state access areas. Additionally, some legitimate access points on private land also exist. There is 11.3 miles of public fishing easements on the lower river. This covers most of the water from the lower reservoir to Pulaski. The area through the village is comprised of a combination of village and privately-controlled property. There is no restrictions on public access down to the Douglaston Salmon Run. The lower river is open all year to trout and salmon fishing.

On September 15, 1994, the upper fly fishing only section was opened through the cooperation of the DEC, Niagara Mohawk and Trout Unlimited. Along with identifying and promoting the need for new fly fishing water, Trout Unlimited used their own funds to help finance a parking lot. This lot is located along County Route 22 and provides easy access via a short path to the river. This upper section begins at a marked boundary at the lower end of the Lighthouse Hill tailrace. It proceeds approximately 0.6 miles to a marked boundary upstream of the fish hatchery.

The bottom of the tailrace represents a small pool that holds migrating fish. There are also some nice size resident,

The lower fly fishing section leading into the Cemetery Pool.

◆

holdover trout in this area. Moving downstream there is only one other pool, but it is a real beauty. It is located toward the lower boundary of the section. The pool is long and has a gentle sweeping current. The whole length of the pool represents excellent holding water, especially along the far side where the river runs along a bank strengthened by a heavy growth of hardwoods. Most of the remaining water is fast and fairly straight, and at first glance appears to offer little angling opportunity. However, with further inspection, pockets and seams formed by bottom or bank structure identify certain holding water. Though, some of the better looking pockets and seams are best fished from the north side, it is very difficult to cross the river in this section, even in low current flows.

The upper fly fishing section is open annually from April 1 through November 30. It is closed in late fall to protect and provide adequate space for bald eagles wintering along the river the past several years.

◆

The Salmon River flowing at two units of water.

The lower fly fishing section was established in 1989. It runs from a marked boundary at Beaverdam Brook, a tributary to the lower Salmon, down approximately 1/4 mile to the County Route 52 bridge. Beginning with a short flow of riffles, the remainder of the section is blessed with a near continuous run of quality holding water. There are two major pools that can hold large concentrations of fish. The first is the Cemetary Pool, located in the top half of the section. It is deep and dark, holding the promise of a large fish with every cast. The second is the Bridge Pool, of which the lower end marks the boundary for this section.

A beautiful run leads into the Cemetary Pool, and can hold good numbers of fish all along the south bank. Fish can also position themselves in the thinner water on the north side of the river, so anglers should take caution before wading and fish the close water first. Another quality run can be found from the tail of the Cemetary Pool down to the Bridge Pool. In low water the lower part of this run is mainly riffle water. But these riffles, as well as those located at the top of the section, can hold both migrating salmon and steelhead.

The lower fly fishing section can be accessed from the County Route 52 bridge. There is a New York state parking lot across County Route 52 along the north bank of the river to be used by wading anglers. The lower section is open annually from September 15 to May 15.

During the respective open season, the fly fishing sections can be fished from 1/2 hour before sunrise to 1/2 hour after sunset. This is catch and release water and currently represents the only no-kill, fly fishing water in New York state. Legal tackle is limited to:

- Traditional fly fishing rod, reel, and line.
- Single artificial flies having one hook point with a 1/2 inch gap maximum.
- Weighted artificial flies allowed.
- Maximum leader length including tippet is 15 feet.
- The maximum distance between the fly and any added weight is four feet.

Note: Fly tackle regulations are being refined through public consultation. Check regulations before fishing.

Since the opening of the lower fly fishing section, I have fished it many hours. Its character and size is perfect for fly fishing and can hold tremendous numbers of fish. Through late fall and winter, it is almost a given that there will be some steelhead found here, sometimes in incredible concentrations. The down side is that this water has become very popular and consequently heavily pressured at times, especially in early to mid fall. Additionally, some steelhead located in this area have been in the river for a good period of time, resulting in stale fish difficult to get to take a fly. This can lead to frustrating fishing. Small flies and light tippets can help the problem, but are not always the answer.

There is a whole river below these special sections which is suitable for fly fishing. Many fly fishers seem intimidated by its size or possibly its less defined holding water. However, by utilizing some of the innovative techniques developed on the

Good fly fishing for steelhead can be found well into May.

◆

Salmon River, most of it can be fly fished successfully. Reading and fishing the water throughout its length is the key to a quality experience on the Salmon River. Be willing to move around. A movement of fresh fish can allow one area of the river to fish better than another on a particular day. Don't let expectations exceed reality. A handful of hookups is a good day on the Salmon River. Do your best to take advantage of the opportunities by landing those hooked. The best advice for landing one in the swift currents of the river is to keep as close to the fish as you can and follow it wherever possible until it tires. Try to find some slack water for finishing the fight.

The lower river is controlled by releases from the hydro-generation dams operating on the river. This causes fluctuations which can have a significant impact on fishing conditions most apparent below the lower fly fishing area. Normal water releases provide for levels which allow a high percentage of the river to be fly fished effectively. Along the river you will hear anglers and merchants speaking of "gates" or "units" of water. This has traditionally been used as the measure of flow and relates to the current discharge mechanism of the generation dam. In terms of cubic feet per second (cfs), the standard one unit of water at peak efficiency is approximately 750 cfs. One-half unit of water would then equate to 375 cfs and two gates would be 1,500 cfs. Flows can be found at this range of levels,

fall through spring. This illustrates the wide fluctuations that can be encountered on a trip to the river. The Salmon is an entirely different river at 350 cfs than it is at 1,500 cfs.

The standard one-half unit gives the river good definition and clearly distinguishes typical holding water. It also provides for easy wading and levels that allow most of the river to be worked with a fly rod. At one unit this begins to change slightly. Wading can become more difficult in some water. The river loses a little of its definition, but good holding water can still be deciphered. The advantage is that some water that is too thin to hold fish at one-half unit can become prime water at one unit. Quality pocket water and long runs are now created. Pools are made larger and the areas where fish can comfortably hold increase significantly. This creates the ability to spread out anglers throughout the river.

At two units the river demonstrates a tremendous change in its character. Much of the definition of the holding water is lost and the river becomes difficult or even dangerous to wade. At this flow the fly fisher needs to be more selective as to the water to be fished. Some of it will be difficult to fish with stan-

Following page: Looking downstream from the County Route 2A bridge.

The main street through the village of Pulaski.

◆

dard techniques and modifications will be required. Other areas may be nearly impossible for the fly rod. Learning quality holding water that can be fished under varying flows is very important when developing a strategy for a day's fishing on the Salmon and many times can be the key to success.

The constant in the equation of water flow is that in recent years a plan has been developed for controlled releases. A group effort between Niagara Mohawk, the DEC, local merchants, and community members has resulted in a committee which has established and monitors a policy for a planned flow. The current policy sets forth minimum water releases for the prime fishing months. In the late 1980s, Niagara Mohawk acknowledged a responsibility to provide a more controlled in-stream flow environment for the fishery. This initiated the formation of the current committee. The result was safer fishing conditions and consistent patterns for fish activity. All changes of flows are made at midnight and it takes about five hours for the full impact of an increase to be felt throughout the river. Presently, fishing is allowed from 1/2 hour before sunrise to 1/2 hour after sunset, from August 15 to March 15, on the lower river below the fly fishing areas. During this period of time the increase in flow occurs prior to any anglers being present on the river.

Under this current experimental plan, the minimum flows for September through November and March 1st to May 15th

will be 550 cfs from midnight to noon and 350 cfs from noon to midnight. For December through February the flows are 400 cfs from midnight to noon and 300 cfs from noon to midnight. The variable here with in-stream flows is that heavy rains or run-off can force greater releases. Additionally, flows can increase through the uncontrolled run-off of feeder streams and storm drains. Conversely, if emergency low water levels are experienced, there are provisions in the plan which would allow for less than the minimum releases. Niagara Mohawk provides a telephone number which is updated after 5 p.m. giving the flow for the next day.

Increases in the stream flow, either through planned releases or run-off, can stimulate fish migration, provided the timing is right. There is no hard and fast rule, but movements of fish can most likely be tied more to increases in flow than any other factor. Activating the fish is the main reason behind greater releases in the morning hours under the plan.

Currently, Niagara Mohawk is in the process of obtaining a license from the Federal Energy Regulatory Commission for continued operation of the power generation facility. Recreational opportunity and environmental protection are important components of the license agreement. This has many potential benefits for the future of the Salmon River. One is a new schedule for minimum in-stream flows. This would provide cool water releases in the summer months and effectively turn the river into a 12 month fishery. The new plan would result in flows of 285 cfs for January through April, 185 cfs May through August, and 335 cfs September through December. It is estimated that the agreement will be completed by April of 1995. New equipment would be required to maintain this flow schedule. It is anticipated that the installation of the equipment would be completed by September of 1996.

Because of its heavy current coupled with slippery rocks and large boulders, the river deserves a healthy respect when it is waded. Some water can be deceivingly difficult to wade or cross, even if it looks fairly shallow. Some type of stream cleat is highly recommended for extra grip on the rocks. Not only do

◆

A clearly displayed access permit is required to fish the Douglaston Salmon Run.

A fall steelhead is subdued after a lengthy struggle.

◆

stream cleats grip the rocks, they are nearly a must on ice and snow. Straight felt soles will freeze in cold weather and result in treacherous footing. The down side of cleats is that they cause some gouging and scraping of the rocks in and along the river. Care should be exercised to minimize this effect. Another piece of equipment which is important for safe wading is a staff. It provides stability, especially in heavy flows. Safety should be a primary concern when fishing the river.

Directly below the lower fly fishing section, the river seems to have a slightly wider appearance but at the same time keeps its intimate personality. The river maintains this characteristic downstream to the point where it is joined by Orwell Brook. This intimate nature creates the type of water that can be readily fly fished. For this reason it is a favored section of mine and deserves special attention.

There is a long run below the County Route 52 bridge. The run plus the long, fast tail comprised of riffles and pockets is prime holding water. This area is accessed using the same lot as the lower fly fishing area. It is probably best fished from the north side. This area receives a fair amount of pressure but there is a good degree of water. Any pockets, caused by large rocks or boulders, can hold fish, especially fall steelhead. It is important to read the water closely. Look for any visible slicks on the surface which indicate that the main current is being deflected creating a pocket. The current behind a rock or boul-

der can be very slow or nonexistent, even in the middle of very heavy flows. This provides perfect holding water for fish on the move or those that have vacated popular pools because of fishing pressure.

Below this run there are two known pools that seem to hold at least some fish at all times. Moving downstream, the first is Schoolhouse Pool and the next is Wire Pool. Both are deep and fairly slow moving. They both hold good numbers of fish in the winter. For fly fishing, one-half unit of water allows them to be fished best. There is the opportunity to utilize some traditional techniques in this area. However, the best opportunities for fly fishing, especially in the fall, is to fish the riffle water at the heads of these pools. It is amazing the fast, shallow water that fish will be found in at this time of year.

These pools can be fished from either side of the river. I prefer the north side by following the path along the river. South side access can be gained by walking the edge of a field near the intersection of County Route 52 and Tar Hill Road. Both of these pools along with the run below the County Route 52 bridge afford good opportunity to play and land even the hottest of fish.

Below these two pools is a nice, narrow stretch of water referred to as Frazier's Run. It consists of some faster water at the head and leads into a long run and tailout. Fish on the move rest here while on their journey. It may not provide the

Brian Slavinski poses with a fresh Chinook salmon taken early in the run in the Douglaston area.

---

same level of winter holding water as does the above, but it's perfect fly fishing water. It is best accessed by walking upstream from the New York state access point at Ellis Cove located on County Route 52.

The Ellis Cove area represents a set of pools, runs and pockets that are some of the finest fly fishing water on the river. The first run is located just upstream from the parking lot. The river makes a bend which is reinforced by large boulders where the river pushes up along the road. This run is normally fished from the south side. However, it may be more effectively approached from along the boulders to adequately cover the holding water at the top of the run without making the fish aware of your presence.

Below this, the Salmon can be accessed by a path along the river. The sharp bends found in this area create some perfect small holding pools. It is also fairly narrow so that the entire river can be covered quite easily. The pools on the bends should be fished from the inside. Crossing the river is required to fish two of the pools. There are nice current seams along the bend pools which define optimum areas for fish to position themselves.

There is a high concentration of gravel in the Ellis Cove area. This provides easy fishing and also lends itself to a high degree of spawning activity in the fall and spring. Pacific salmon on spawning beds represent the opportunity to take advantage of their aggressive and territorial behavior. At this time they can be regularly caught on a fly. I tend to steer away from fishing to steelhead on their beds, however. Since they will return to the lake and potentially spawn again, I feel it is more sporting to let them go about their business. So in the spring I concentrate on fresh run fish moving up or dropbacks that have successfully spawned. Steelhead dropping to the lake will normally be on the take. The Ellis Cove area has shown to be good water to pursue dropbacks which can be present well into May.

Below Ellis Cove the nature of the river changes dramatically. It is very narrow and takes on a channelized character. The flow is fairly quick. This type of water lacks obvious definition, but fish can be found holding throughout its length. Traditional back casting is impossible due to high banks and overhanging brush and trees. Roll casting or slip casting becomes the only way to fish this area with a fly. Try to select a section that appears to have some current breaks or structure which will encourage fish to hold next to or below it. Although drift boats will commonly stop and fish throughout, the pressure from wading anglers is normally low since this stretch is a fair walk from the Ellis Cove parking lot. One disadvantage of this section is that the heavy current of the channelized flow does make for a difficult situation when it comes to playing and landing fish.

Ominous skies of late fall provide the backdrop as a lone angler fishes the head of Frazier's Run.

The lower Black Hole in September.

◆

Just downriver from this channelized flow enters Orwell Brook, a main tributary to the Salmon. At this point the river has travelled approximately three miles from the lower reservoir. Orwell Brook is a good size stream and receives a fair number of fish in the fall and spring. It also sees a steady amount of fishing pressure at this time as well. Orwell Brook can be legally fished, however, in fall and spring the opportunity is mainly for fish that have entered the stream to spawn. Since there is a significant level of natural reproduction occurring here, it is a good idea to leave these fish alone to help propagate the future resource and protect wild fish.

Orwell Brook seems to again change the river's complexion, it now has more volume and begins to spread out. The next approximately six and a half miles to Pulaski represent a certain challenge to the fly fisher. Some pools are wide and deep, making effective coverage with a fly rod difficult. However, most can be fly fished as long as the proper technique is matched to the water. Reading and understanding the water in this stretch is critical. Areas that are referred to as pools or holes are not as obvious as those found on Pacific steelhead or Atlantic salmon rivers. There is not always the classic riffle leading into a pool which gradually tapers into a tailout. Instead many of the pools are comprised of deeper depressions or slots in the river with

Previous page: Looking up at the riffles and pockets found below the Interstate 81 bridge. Photo by Jerry Senecal.

gentle riffles at their head. The good holding water may not always be visible at first glance. Most of it needs to be fished to get a feel for the best lies.

There is good access to the river throughout this section. Starting upstream, New York state access points and parking lots are found at the Trestle Pool on both sides of the river, at the County Route 48 bridge in Pineville and Sportman's Pool on both sides of the river. A county access point is located at the County Route 2A bridge just up from Pulaski. Drift boat access for the lower river can be found at the County Route 52 bridge, the County Route 48 bridge, the County Route 2A bridge, in the village off Forest Drive and at the estuary. The Trestle Pool, Sportman's Pool, and Compactor Pool above County Route 2A are examples of some of the deeper pools in this section. The riffles and pockets leading into each can be easily covered with a fly rod.

There are some popular pools and runs that are made for fly fishing in this section. The area near Pineville offers prime water. The pockets and depressions of the Refrigerator Hole upstream from Pineville is one of the best known fly fishing spots on this part of the river. In addition, the stretch of water above the Compactor Pool and just below the County Route 2A bridge provides very good opportunity.

Some of the best fly fishing water can be found between the more well known or named pools. Again riffle water and pockets should all be investigated. In reality this type of water may hold more fish than the deep pools, especially in the fall. Two examples of lesser known runs, perfect for fly fishing, come to mind. A sharp bend below the Trestle Pool is the first and is best fished from the north side of the river. It is a short walk from the north access point of the Trestle Pool. The other is a pretty run just above Sportman's Pool. The river narrows some at its head and creates more of a small traditional pool. It is best fished from the south side of the river.

Above Sportsman's Pool another main tributary of the Salmon, Trout Brook, feeds into the river. Good reproduction is also experienced in its headwaters.

The double bridge where Interstate 81 crosses the river marks the beginning of yet another change in its character. The Salmon flows out of a surrounding that shows very little change by man along its banks into an area where some development has occurred. The river curves and winds its way through Pulaski for nearly two and a half miles creating a special opportunity to catch trophy-size fish while amidst the confines of a quaint little village.

Another special feature is that this stretch of the river offers a tremendous amount of fly fishing water. Beginning below the big pool at the Interstate 81 bridge, there is a long series of heavy rapids. Salmon and steelhead can be found throughout. The key is reading the water, determining the pockets and getting the fly down to the fish in a quick efficient manner. This water can be accessed from the parking lot behind Tony's Salmon Country Sport Shop.

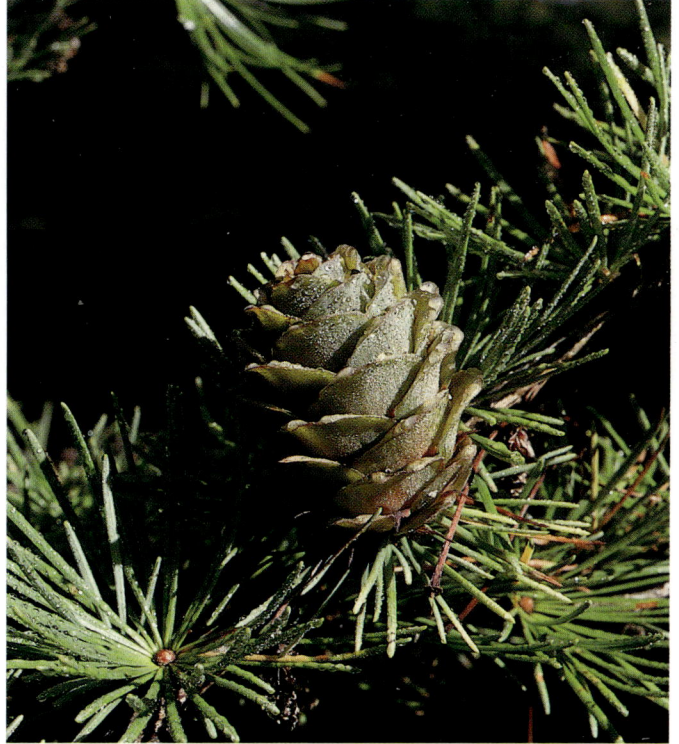
Tamarak adds color to the river bank. Photo by Bill Reed.

◆

The historic Selkirk Lighthouse.

Below these rapids are two nice runs. The first is classic steelhead holding water. Parking is available near the pool at the ball park lot off Dunbar Road on the south side of the river. Here a long glide with a gradual current seam flows over a mix of gravel and boulders. This water is a pleasure to fish. Below this there is another short slot or run which is the preferred resting water for fish on the move.

From here down to the first bridge in town, or the "short bridge" as it is referred to, there is more pocket water. Some of it is extremely fast and heavy. Do not be intimidated. Pick out the pockets and fish it diligently. The obvious problem with this water is landing fish in the heavy flows. Try to force the fish upriver during the fight.

A beautiful, long traditional salmon and steelhead pool exists below the short bridge. When water flows are in the one-half to one unit range, most of this pool can be easily fly fished. The tail of the pool is especially appealing. Heavy rapids below it require a fair effort on the fish's part for passage. Often having run this type of water salmon and steelhead will rest in the tail of the first slower current they reach. The tail of this pool offers respite for fish on the move. Another positive aspect is that there are many large rocks and boulders throughout, especially in the tail, which create structure that encourages fish to hold for a longer period of time. The pool is best fished from the left side looking downstream. Access can be gained by parking in the village.

Below the pool at the short bridge the quality fly fishing water continues. The river makes a sweeping bend to the right and is filled with the previously mentioned heavy rapids. This equates into more pocket water worth exploring. This flows into the long, slow, gentle roll of the pool above the "long bridge". This water has some fly fishing application, mostly in lower water flows. The Salmon then moves into what is probably the best known set of pocket water on the river. It is referred to as the Staircase Run. It is a classic mix of riffles and pockets, each holding the possibility of a fish.

There is only one other pool below this point where there is public access. This is the famous Black Hole. It is an amazingly deep area of the river. Although decent fly fishing water can only be found in the very tail of the pool, it is an interesting piece of water to observe in order to gain a full sense of the river's capacity and power.

Below the Black Hole and including one run above, the remaining water to the estuary of approximately two and a half miles is owned and controlled by the Douglaston Salmon Run. This is private water requiring a daily access permit. Permits can be purchased at the parking lot on County Route 5. The only access to this stretch is via the parking lot. Neatly maintained trails lead from the lot to the river and adds to the pleasure of fishing this water.

All aspects of this operation are very impressive and I have only words of praise for this part of the river. It starts with an ethical philosophy and continues through strong management. The river keepers at the main parking lot monitor conditions and help in any way to make your day on the Douglaston Salmon Run enjoyable. Employees or rangers that walk the river banks are courteous and helpful. They are more than willing to direct you to the safest and easiest trail when traveling to a new section of water. Customers engaging in unethical fishing practices are asked to leave. A hotline, which is updated daily, details fishing and water conditions. Stream cleats are required at certain times of year and a wading staff is recommended.

Since this water is positioned lowest on the river, it offers the angler an advantage. The fish in this section are normally fresh from the lake. The result is typically aggressive fish that are willing to take a fly. This is especially important for Chinook salmon. The condition of these fish deteriorates fairly quickly and they are fished for with intense pressure upriver. Trying to intersect a run of salmon direct from the lake may be the best approach for success. Again, rainfall will generally be

The beauty of fall comes in many forms.

associated with a draw of fish from the lake. Some Chinooks and cohos will exhibit a silver appearance and are incredible fighters, the definitive "chromers". Not all salmon caught in this section are silver, some darken in the lake or estuary before their movement up the river.

My initiation to the Douglaston Salmon Run came a number of years ago when I luckily came upon some fresh Chinooks along with a sprinkling of brown trout. The salmon I hooked were very strong. As their silver bodies glistened in the sunshine, I realized this was a type of fly fishing for Chinook that I had not experienced before. Even now, after fishing many other rivers, it is apparent that the Douglaston Salmon Run provides some of the best fly fishing opportunity for Chinook salmon to be found throughout the Great Lakes.

The very beginning of the Douglaston Salmon Run includes the run above the Black Hole referred to as the Coho Hole. This is a pool with a heavy set of rapids at its head. The rapids are split by an island. This water does not receive a large amount of pressure since it is such a long walk from the parking lot.

The next two pools down, the Lower Black and The Glide offer significant holding water for steelhead. The Glide is prime fly fishing water where a variety of techniques can be successful. The glassy surface current of The Glide runs over a pool of moderate depth. Included in the pool are deeper slots which attract fish, especially under heavy pressure.

The next named pool is The Wall. This is an interesting series of heavy water defined by large pockets and eddies. Since it is close to the parking lot it is a popular area to fish. There is also a good run of pocket water above The Wall.

Fly fishing opportunity abounds all through the remaining water. The Flats, just below The Wall, serves as a quality holding area. Deeper grooves within its moderate depth is the preferred water to present a fly. Downstream, a number of channels and islands characterize the make-up of the river. The Spring Hole below has similar qualities to The Flats but in general is not as deep. It is ideal water to cover with a fly rod.

A couple of these islands push a good portion of the main flow through a narrow area along the north bank. The result is two nice intimate pools. The first is the Joss Hole and below this is the Clay Hole. Both hold fish. During the salmon run, Chinooks will normally be found in the heavy water at the head of the holes.

Below the Clay Hole, the force of the current lessens. This helps to form a string of pools that offer the best opportunity on the river for traditional fly fishing techniques. The Meadow Run, Bus Hole and Lower Clay Hole all possess a gentler flow and adequate depth to hold fish. Since predominantly fresh fish will be found in this water, they are more likely to respond to a fly fished in a traditional manner.

In between the named waters are numerous runs, slots, pocket water and side channels, all of which can be productive. Do not overlook the pockets, no matter how small. Fish each with the confidence that it holds a fish. The key throughout the river is to read and fish the water.

From here the river moves into the estuary which is about a mile and a half in length. This portion of the river is highlighted with a distinguishing landmark, the Selkirk Lighthouse. This structure was built in 1838 to assist the great trade opportunities provided by the waters of Lake Ontario. The lighthouse still stands strong today and is a point of interest for any visitor to the area. Some fly fishing possibilities exist in the estuary from a float tube or small boat. The best option may be for the Chinook salmon that stack up in the estuary prior to their ascent up the river. Warm water species can be caught in the spring and summer as well.

A River of Seasons

The Northeast portion of the United States is blessed with the beauty of changing seasons. This is a characteristic that adds to the diversity of the Salmon River. Each season has its own attraction and appeal, giving the river a variety of appearances throughout the year.

◆

Fishing for winter steelhead.

Some guides feel that a drift boat provides the best way to fish the Salmon.

Late summer and early fall is viewed by most as the beginning of the Salmon River season. The large runs of migrating trout and salmon, coupled with comfortable air temperatures, bring many anglers to the river. In late August and September the river is lined with fertile plant life and green trees. Most days can be fished in light clothing and summer weight waders. Weather conditions are typically dry, causing the flows to adhere to scheduled minimum releases.

In late September and October, the river begins to change its look almost daily. The hardwoods show a constant progression of color. Greens give way to brilliant hues of yellow, orange and red. It is as though Mother Nature is painting a picture, with the trees as her canvas. The combination of colors reaches it crescendo in the middle of October and it is wonderful to be on the river. This time of year also brings with it the promise of the first major movement of the true prize to the serious angler, fresh run steelhead.

In late October the leaves that provided such an artistic outline of the river can now become the fly fisher's curse. Windy days remove the dead and dying leaves from the trees and deposit them in the river. Heavy rain can have the same result as the rising water gathers fallen leaves along the river bank. This makes for difficult to nearly impossible fishing, as leaves are hooked on nearly every cast. The leaves seem to also cause the fish to lie low and avoid anything that is drifting in the water, including a well presented fly. This situation can correct itself quickly, as the next day can bring a reduction in floating leaves and fish that are willing to respond.

Previous page: Anglers prospect the numerous pockets found in the lower river.

In November most of the leaves have fallen and the river now seems naked. It has the appearance of being wider, since shoreline that was recently blocked by dense foliage is now visible. This is my favorite time to be on the Salmon. Good numbers of steelhead can normally be found and temperatures can be quite comfortable. However, there is almost always a chill in

Cozy quarters can be a welcome sight after a long, cold day on the river.

the air, an indication of winter's fury soon to come.

Once the calendar reaches December the landscape is likely to change again. Snowy conditions make a frequent visit to the Salmon River area. Actually, this part of New York receives the state's largest amount of annual snowfall. This is mainly the result of a weather phenomenon referred to as lake affect snow. Cold winter air sweeping across the warmer waters of Lake Ontario picks up moisture and drops it on land in the form of snow. Weather conditions can change quickly in January and February. Sunny periods can turn into snow squalls in the blink of an eye. Air temperatures can be brutal. I normally attempt timing visits to the river when tolerable temperatures are forecasted.

Winter is a time for solitude on the river. Finding stretches with little or no fishing pressure becomes easy. Many times you find yourself alone with a pool of steelhead. Newly fallen snow creates a hush over the river. It provides a peacefulness and serenity that is unique to the winter months.

Dressing for the elements becomes critical in the winter. A pair of insulated boot foot waders are a must. So is a warm, weatherproof shell. Loose layers of fleece and wool should be worn underneath. Underwear that wicks away moisture from the body is very important for cold weather fishing. The extremities also need proper attention. A warm hat reduces heat loss and a pair of gloves can keep hands comfortable and functioning.

When I think of winter, a number of outings on the Salmon come to mind. One particular day stands out. Temperatures were in the low twenties, but with no wind and sunshine hitting the water, it felt much warmer. The ice that continually formed in the guides served as a constant reminder that it wasn't. Though I have not found the total solution to this problem, lower diameter fly lines and adding water repellant solutions to the guides of the rod do help. Steelhead can be a little sluggish in the winter, but a fresh run fish can exhibit tremendous energy. One silver bullet was about to take me into my backing, but the knot between the fly line and backing would not pass through the ice-filled guide, spelling disaster. Luckily, there were more willing fish in the river. There are not many better ways to spend a winter's day.

Spring rains and run-off define the expected conditions in March and April. However, the line between winter and spring is never clearly defined on the Salmon River. Substantial snow storms can be experienced into April. Flows will typically be high and strong, and two units of water at this time can be expected. As the melting snow disappears along the river, keeping the water cold, the refreshing hope that winter conditions will soon be left behind now prevails.

Trees along the river begin to show life again in May. Warm weather returns. Late run steelhead as well as post spawn fish provide the quarry. With raising water tempera-

Guide Fran Verdoliva assisting a future fly fishing enthusiast.

tures the fish can be quite active. By June and July everything is green. The best fishing opportunities are found on the upper river for stream-bred trout. Temperatures can be hot during the day but are normally cool in the evening providing great weather for camping near the river.

Faces of the River

Many individuals have had a positive impact on the Salmon River. From a fly fishing standpoint, one particular person stands out. Fran Verdoliva has guided on the river for approximately 15 years and was the first to specialize in fly fishing. His early efforts found that traditional techniques and patterns worked quite well in low water. But in the early days water releases were not controlled and wide fluctuations caused difficult situations. Fran developed techniques for various conditions. His running line method, which he stumbled upon after he lost a shooting head to the bottom of the river, has enabled anglers to fish deep slots and high water. The technique was probably first discovered in the Midwest, but Fran has refined it to meet the demands of the Salmon River. He has also worked extensively with light tippets and soft rods which handle them best. Using some of his discoveries, Fran lays claim to the IGFA fly fishing record for a steelhead caught on two pound test tippet—16 pounds and 8 ounces! Fran works very hard for his clients and attempts to provide the type of experience that first attracted him to the river.

Today Fran is attempting to convey a different message. He would like to see each angler accept a certain responsibility, to not just take but to give something back to the river. He suggests that each individual should be a "steward of the river" with the objective of creating a consideration for fellow anglers and establishing an environment where everyone can enjoy the quality of the fishery.

Another individual who has helped shape the river as we know it today is Douglas Barclay. He owns and operates the Douglaston Salmon Run on land that has seen nine generations of his family. Mr. Barclay is known by many as a former state senator. He feels strongly about the quality of the Salmon and that such a great river should have a full dedication to sport fishing. This belief prompted the establishment of the private fishing area that is a great alternative to shutting off access to the public. Mr. Barclay is a staunch supporter of river improve-

Jerry Kustich releases a 13 pound steelhead that took a slowly drifted fly.

The slower, gentle flow of the lower Douglaston Salmon Run.

◆

ment and hopefully his influence will be felt well into the future.

In an official capacity, the actions of the DEC, along with community involvement, has resulted in the tremendous fishing opportunity that exists today. In particular, Les Wedge, Regional Fisheries Manager and Cliff Creech, Natural Resource Supervisor, have been important players in the development of the salmon and steelhead fisheries in Lake Ontario, with a particular emphasis on the Salmon River. Both have been involved in the current salmonid program practically from the beginning. Early on, the potential of the fishery was recognized. In order for this potential to be realized, substantial river access acquired into perpetuity became a main objective. This is exactly what the DEC has done through the involvement of Les and Cliff, and is evidenced by the vast miles of public fishing easements. Along with continuous fishery management decisions, attention is now focused on improving the sport fishing on the Salmon River. Les sees education as the key. The DEC has just completed an educational video aimed at increasing the awareness of anglers and the community. The next goal for Les and Cliff is to extend the lower river to a year-round fishery.

In 1994, the river lost one of its true friends. Gary Johnson, guide and creative fly tier, died after a battle with a long illness. I never had the pleasure to fish with Gary, but those that did tell stories of his expertise and love for the river. He displayed a code of ethics that should serve as a model for us all. Gary will be missed by many.

There is a vast myriad of services found along or near the river designed to enhance a trip to the area. Eating establishments range from diners to fast food chains to relaxing restaurants. There are also a variety of taverns where one can unwind after a long day on the river. Lodging at very reasonable rates can be found throughout the area. A stay at one of the inns designed to service fly fishing anglers can help complete the experience while at the Salmon River. The Fish Inn Post in Altmar near the fly fishing areas and the Wild River Inn in Port Ontario near the Douglaston Salmon Run offer comfortable lodging with a cozy sitting room where guests can make friends and share experiences. The Sportman's Lodge and Double Eagle Lodge in Pulaski also offer this type of atmosphere. The Douglaston Manor Lodge operates two beautiful farmhouses that can be rented by groups of anglers. Fort

Coho salmon can be aggressive and take a fly well.

◆

Geronimo in Redfield provides rustic accommodations and easy access to the upper river and reservoir. Lodging can also be found in more of a hotel setting at The Portly Angler, Redwood Motel, Tony's Salmon Country Lodge and Hotel, and Whitaker's Motel.

Though the Salmon River can easily be fished on your own, a good guide can make all the difference in the world. There are a number of quality guides operating in the Salmon River area and it is important to select one that has a solid reputation and years of experience on the river. A good guide should provide a learning experience as well as the best opportunity to catch fish under the given conditions. For fly fishing it is important that the guide has a knowledge of the variety of techniques required to meet the specific situations presented by the river.

Many feel that the best way to fish the river is with a drift boat. This provides access to much more water than can be walked in a day. It is also a great way to see the river, to view its diversity and beauty, along with providing a relaxing and enjoyable experience. There are a number of guides that have years of experience with this approach. They also offer walk-in trips. This list includes Kent Appleby, Dave Barber of the Fish Inn Post, Troy Creasy, Bill Markle, and Todd Sheltra of the Wild River Inn.

Fly Fishing the Salmon River

The fly tackle requirements for fishing the lower Salmon River are quite simple. Seven and eight weight rods are a good match for steelhead and brown trout, while eight and nine weight rods are the right choice for Chinook salmon. Some guides prefer five and six weight rods for steelhead to better accommodate very light tippets. Rod length is important for proper line control. It should be a minimum of nine feet. My preference is a ten foot rod. The main characteristic of the reel is a smooth, adjustable drag. There should be no hesitation in the drag when a fish takes line from the spool. This is important to handle the start and stop fight of a steelhead. The adjustable drag provides flexibility when using light tippets or for fighting fish in confined areas.

Extra spools allow for adjusting to the water conditions. Each spool should have a minimum of 150 yards of backing. I carry a weight forward floating line, a floating running line, and a couple of sink-tips. Leaders for floating lines vary in length from six to 15 feet, depending on water depth and current speed. Normally they will be in the ten to 12 foot range. Leaders for sink-tips will be considerably shorter, typically about two to three feet. Tippet size and length will be determined by water conditions and the quarry. 1/0X and 0X is

King Salmon   Polar Shrimp   Skunk
Woolly Bugger   Pink STS Spey   Salmon   River Smolt
Green Butt Woolly Worm Black and Lite-Brite Stonefly Goldribbed Hare's Ear Fluorescent Stonefly Nymph Chironomid
Flea   Frammus   Krystal Egg   Glo Bug   Estaz Egg   Med-A-Egg

required for salmon. 1X down to 4X will cover most conditions for steelhead. Abrasion resistant material is very important since the river's rocks and large boulders can wreak havoc on one's leader.

It is essential to understand that the fish migrating into the lower Salmon will generally be positioned on or near the bottom. This will have a direct impact on the successful presentation of the fly. When using floating lines, weight will normally be added to the leader to get the fly in the strike zone. Either split shot or slinky rigs are used. My preference is split shot which provides for easy adjustment. The distance from the weight to the fly will range from two to four feet. I add my split shot utilizing a tag end off the knot between leader and tippet. The tag of about two inches, with an overhand knot at the end, acts as a dropper. Low diameter leaders create less surface area which improves the natural drift of the fly and should be used with any technique that utilizes a floating line. The result can be gained by tying your own to meet the specific situation.

A wide variety of techniques can be employed based on water conditions and angler preference. Due to the river's generally heavy current flow, certain techniques perform better than others. The basic presentation is a dead drift or standard nymphing technique. A weight forward line is combined with a long leader, weight and a high-floating strike indicator attached near the junction of the leader and fly line. This is best used in

A clump of wild mushrooms.

◆

small pools, runs, pockets and seams of moderate current that can be approached within ten to twenty feet. The cast is made up and across stream. A tuck cast will allow the fly to hit the water and begin to sink before the fly line comes in contact with the surface of the river. The line is properly mended to attain a slow drift. A movement of the strike indicator contrary to the current will signal a take or the rig being lodged on the bottom. If the latter happens frequently, an adjustment to the weight is required.

For heavy runs and slots, fast pockets, and pools, I remove the strike indicator and fish by feel. With fast runs and pockets it is critical to get the weight and fly through the heavy surface current and down to the fish quickly. Adequate weighting is essential. Unsuccessful anglers commonly fail to get the fly down to the fish. Do not be intimidated by casting weight on the leader. To do so eliminates the ability to fly fish some of the river's most productive water. The back cast should be allowed to straighten out fully before beginning a slow open forward stroke. Also there will be many situations where roll casting will be sufficient or required. Be sure that the weight on the leader is at the water's surface before the cast is begun. Again, the cast is made up and across. Occasionally contact with the bottom should be felt. The take of a fish will normally come in the manner of a sharp interruption of the anticipated drift. The fly is allowed to drift just below the casting position. This technique can be used to cover water that is 30 feet or so away and can also be effective where it is possible to wade very close to holding water, typical of heavy pockets. In this case there may only be five to ten feet of fly line past the tip of the rod. The fly line normally does not come in contact with the surface. The drift is short and quick. It is also incredibly effective.

◆

Utilizing a floating line and a long leader is a common set-up.

The Fish Inn Post.

◆

short cut approach to fly fishing. This technique is used by some in all situations without ever learning the proper casting or control of a fly rod. Nonetheless, when matched with the right situation this is a very innovative approach.

There are a few alternatives to this running line technique. For those interested in some of the benefits but prefer traditional casting, lining a seven weight rod with an exaggerated weight forward four or five weight line works quite well. Another option shown to me by guide Lou Baum, is to attach a 30 foot floating shooting head to the running line. This provides the casting of a standard line but reduces line drag when a fish is hooked.

Fast sink-tip lines are effective in some types of water. They are best matched with runs and pools of a moderate to slow current flow. It is important to get the fly down fast. The cast is normally made slightly up and across. Proper mending allows the tip and fly to sink. Takes are determined by feel and will typically come as the fly just begins to swing. Mini tips can be used to fish slower pockets. Lines such as the Teeny T Series and homemade shooting heads added to running lines work best.

Dave Barber displays a large lake-run brown trout.

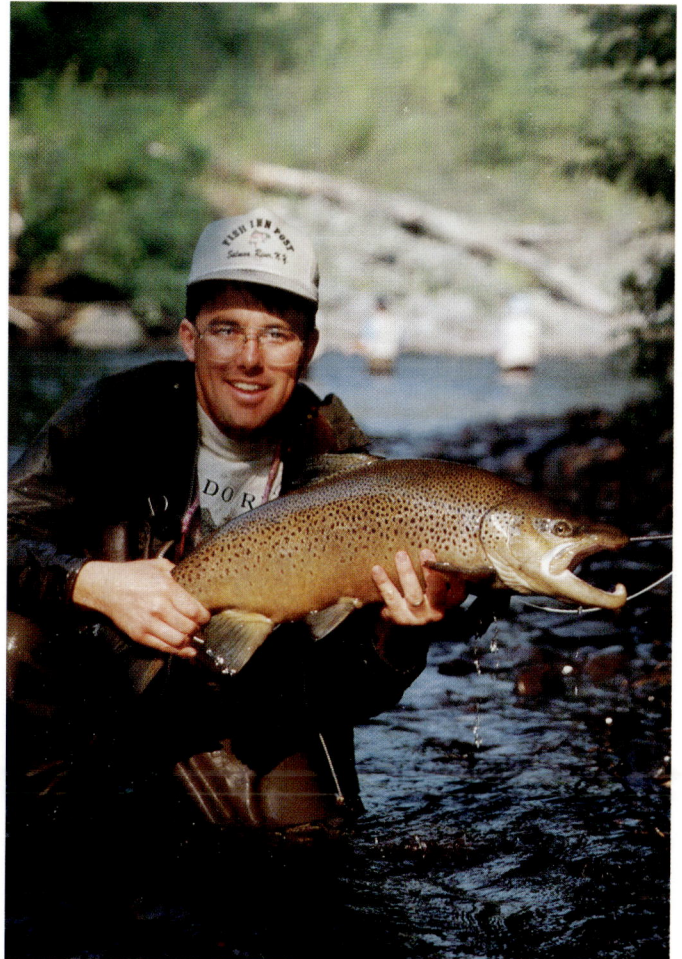

This setup can also be used to fish riffles that lead into a pool. In this situation the fly is allowed to drift and swing slowly through the water. Takes can be hard and forceful.

When fishing large pools, deep slots where close positioning by wading is impossible, and in high water levels in the range of one and a half to two units, certain modifications are a must. Fran Verdoliva has developed and refined a technique to accommodate these factors. It replaces the weight forward line with a .029 inch diameter floating running line as the main fly line. A leader of normally ten to 14 feet is utilized. A hot orange butt section aids in strike detection. Instead of a standard fly cast, a slip cast is used which utilizes the weight of split shot or a slinky added to the leader to propel the fly and to shoot the loose coils of line that have been peeled from the reel. About twenty feet of line and leader is allowed past the rod tip, with the tension of the weight on the leader touching the water's surface to further load the rod, the cast is made up and across. The fly is allowed to drift along the bottom in a near dead drift fashion. Takes are indicated by a stoppage in the drift. For light tippets, Fran prefers soft rods which cushion the fight of the fish. He has developed fly rods produced on noodle rod blanks for this purpose.

This technique has a number of advantages. First, it can cover water that is a great distance from the casting position. Second, is that the low weight of the running line results in very little belly from the rod tip to the water. This provides for better line control and keener contact with the fly. Third, the low diameter of the line allows it to better cut through the heavy currents when fighting a fish and results in less icing of the guides in winter. One disadvantage of this technique is that it has allowed some Salmon River anglers to take a dramatic

nymphs such as a Black Stonefly or the Gold Ribbed Hare's Ear are also top producers, especially when casting to stubborn fish. Two patterns that have produced extremely well for me are the Frammus and the Salmon Flea. Both are easy to tie and combine a body of chenille with Glo Bug yarn. They can be tied in a range of colors from purple to chartreuse, and in sizes f6 to 14. As a rule, smaller flies should be used for stale fish, while fresh, aggressive fish will likely be much less selective.

Woolly Buggers and Comets are top producers for Chinook and coho salmon. They are also good patterns to combine with any technique that allows the fly to swing in the current. Other traditional steelhead patterns such as the Skykomish Sunrise and the Skunk also work well in this capacity. Also a variety of timeless wet flies such as the Mickey Finn and Royal Coachman produce fish. A number of patterns have been designed for the Salmon River. Most incorporate synthetic materials to portray a flashy or life-like appearance. These patterns have mainly been designed and refined by Salmon River guides such as Fran Verdoliva and Greg Liu along with Jim Rusher, owner of Whitaker's Sport Shop. Be sure to check the current regulations with respect to tackle, rigging, and flies.

What the Future Holds

Both concern and optimism characterize the future years for the Salmon River. The concern centers around management and conservation issues in both the river and Lake Ontario. The issue that has drawn the most recent attention has been a reduction of the forage base in the lake. Lower phosphate levels, a result of eliminating this ingredient from detergents, and an exotic species called the zebra mussel, appear to be the main causes. The decrease in phosphates has resulted in a

Maple products are an important source of income throughout the Northeast. Photo by Bill Reed.

Fresh run fall steelhead will often move to a larger pattern tied in a traditional style. Bill Reed photo.

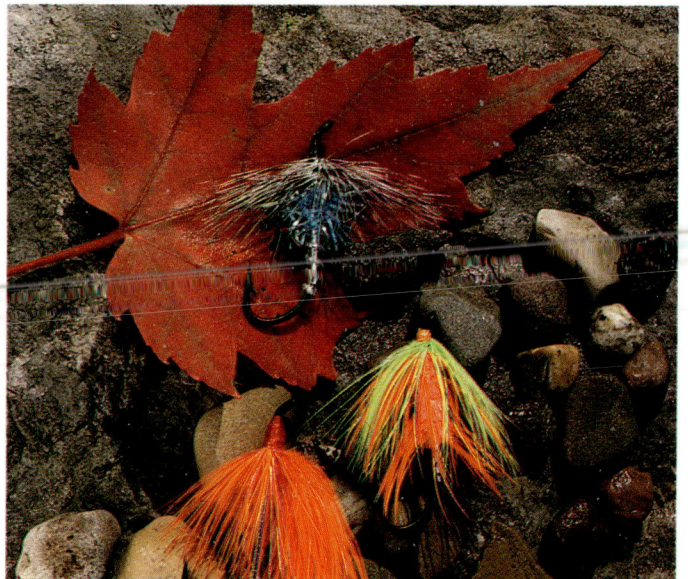

There is also the opportunity to utilize some traditional techniques. Allowing the fly to slowly swing across the current using a floating line or sink-tip is possible. Some of the water found in the Douglaston Salmon Run provides the gentle flows needed for the use of such methods. To be successful with this classic style it is usually important that there be some fresh, aggressive fish present in water that is above 40 degrees.

A wide variety of flies are used to take fish on the Salmon River. Such a variety supports my belief that the presentation of the fly is much more important than the pattern itself. Therefore, a simple fly selection is normally all that is required for success on the lower river.

Egg patterns, nymphs and small wet flies work well with any technique that presents the fly in a naturally drifting fashion. Egg patterns, Glo Bugs or Estaz Eggs in a variety of colors and sizes work well for steelhead and brown trout. Standard

Previous page: Splendid fall colors on the Salmon River.

A large male steelhead before its release.

◆

reduction of the nutrient level of the lake. The zebra mussel is a small shelled creature about the size of a finger nail that siphons nutrients from the water. The combined effect has caused a change in the food chain and decreased the numbers and size of the alewife, the main food source of the Chinook salmon. Future stockings of Chinook will be decreased by nearly sixty-five percent. For the angler fishing the Salmon River, there is a bright side. Steelhead seek a much wider diet and are not affected by this decrease in the same manner. The numbers of planted steelhead will increase slightly and it appears that a greater emphasis will be placed upon the management of this species as well as its importance to the fishery.

Over-harvesting of fish in the lake and river is another problem that prevents this river from reaching its true potential. Catch and release fishing, which is well established in most parts of the country, is only in its infancy on the Salmon River and Lake Ontario. Extremely liberal daily kill limits established at the beginning of the current fishery are outdated and need immediate attention. It is simple common sense that tighter regulations and reduced harvest will have an immediate positive impact on the fishery. The put and take image of the fishery needs to be addressed and changed, especially now, with its decreased forage base, we must get more from less.

Unethical practices continue to be a problem, mainly during the Chinook and coho salmon run. The steelhead seems to attract a sporting group who are concerned with fair play. However, it will take continued education to change attitudes of some during the peak of the salmon season.

Many good things are also happening to the river and the fishery. The previously mentioned licensing agreement should result in cool water releases throughout the summer months. Hopefully, this will provide water temperatures which can attract and hold Skamania strain steelhead during the hottest part of the year. The Atlantic salmon program should also get a boost from the cool water releases. Creating the environment for reproduction in the river along with expansion of the small-mouth bass fishery are other benefits expected from these releases. Time will spell out the true potential of the summer fishery.

Another exciting development has transpired during the past year. As a result of financial considerations and directives from the Public Service Commission, Niagara Mohawk has provided for the sale of some land and easements to the DEC for conservation use. What this means to the fishery is a 200 foot wide conservation easement along most of the lower river to the village of Pulaski, which will preserve its natural beauty and character. It also results in permanent public fishing rights along this same stretch to guarantee the enjoyment of this river for future generations. A comprehensive plan is being developed so that the newly acquired land and easements will benefit all the river's users and visitors.

In this time of change for the Salmon River, the DEC has become involved in many aspects of its management. This has resulted in a very positive situation. Greater involvement by agencies and the general public results in informed recommendations and decisions. Progress always seems to be slowed by the diversity of individuals utilizing the resource, but, today there does seem to be an enlightened emphasis on education and caring for the fishery by many concerned groups.

The Salmon River represents a touch of wilderness in close proximity to so many population centers. It is a river where the quality of the experience is all in what you make it. The opportunity is there and with patience and persistence you can come away with memories that last a lifetime.

The sun sets on a frigid day of steelheading in water located below the Trestle Pool.

Lodges

Double Eagle Lodge
8221 Rome Road
Pulaski, NY 13142
(315) 298-6162

Douglaston Manor Lodge
6871 Port Road
Pulaski, NY 13142
(315) 298-5105 or 6527

Fish Inn Post
River Road, RD1, Box A-1
Altmar, NY 13302
(315) 298-6406

Fort Geronimo Sports Lodge
RR 1, Box 47, McCaw Road
Redfield, NY 13437
(315) 599-7761

Jayhawkers Bunkhouse
CC Road, Box 132
Altmar, NY 13302
(315) 964-2557

Fort Geronimo located along the upper reservoir in Redfield.

A variety of lodging is available.

The Portly Angler
Box 215, Richland
Pulaski, NY 13142
(315) 298-4773

Redwood Motel
Box 315, Routes 13 & I-81
Pulaski, NY 13142
(315) 298-4717

Sportsman's Lodge
County Route 2A, Box 612
Pulaski, NY 13142
(315) 298-5763

Tony's Salmon Country Lodge and Hotel
7621 Rome Road
Pulaski, NY 13142
(315) 298-4104

Whitaker's Motel
7700 Rome Road
Pulaski, NY 13142
(315) 298-6162

Wild River Inn
7977 Route 3, Scenic Highway
Pulaski, NY 13142
(315) 298-4195

Campgrounds

Pineville Campgrounds
RD #4, Route 13
Pulaski, NY 13142
(315) 298-2325

Selkirk Shores State Park
Route 3
Pulaski, NY 13142
(315) 298-5737

Morning dew. Bill Reed photo.

◆

Greater emphasis on steelhead management will be seen in the future on the Salmon River.

A number of shops along the river sell equipment and licenses.

Todd Sheltra
7977 Route 3, Scenic Highway
Pulaski, NY 13142
(315) 298-4195

Fran Verdoliva
PO Box 568
Mexico, NY 13114
(315) 963-3905

Fall is a great time to be on the river.

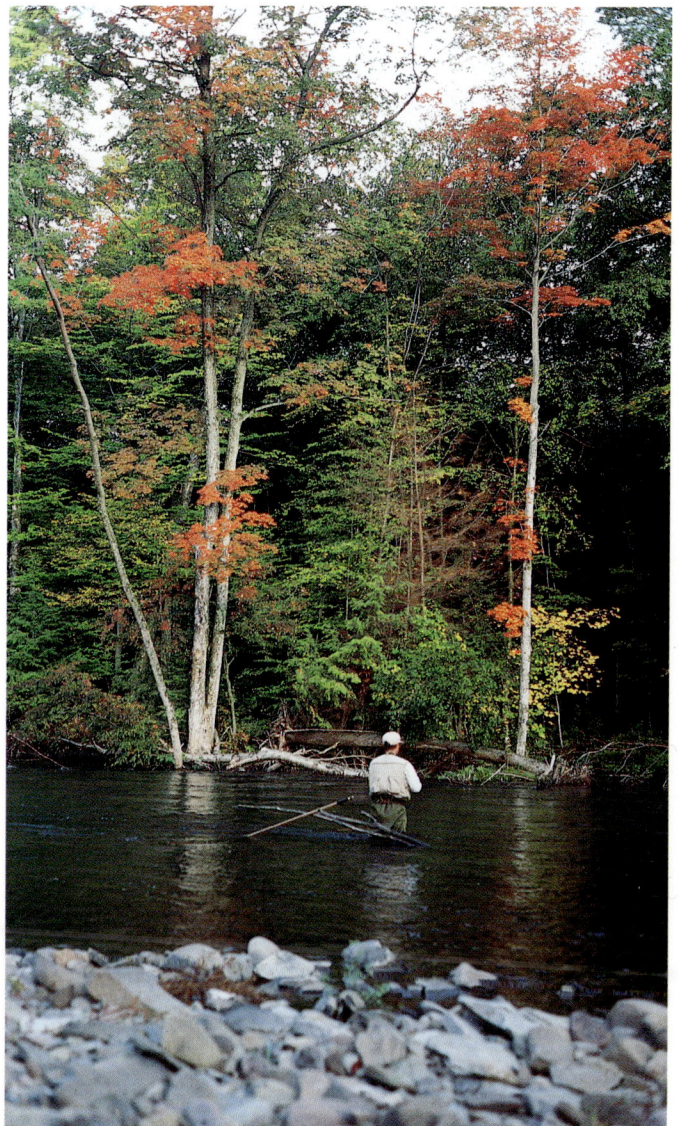

Guides

Kent Appleby
PO Box 462
Pulaski, NY 13142
(315) 298-4371

Dave Barber
River Road, RD 1, Box A-1
Altmar, NY 13302
(315) 298-6406

Lou Baum
20 Roxwell Court
Fairport, NY 14450
(716) 223-8236

Troy Creasy
RD 1, Hager Road
Pulaski, NY 13142
(315) 298-2410
Bill Markle
151 Blount Road
Hastings, NY 13076
(315) 676-3475

Fly Shops

Fish Inn Post Fly & Tackle
River Road, RD 1, Box A-1
Altmar, NY 13302
(315) 298-7775

Tony's Salmon Country Sports
7621 Rome Road
Pulaski, NY 13142
(315) 298-4104

Whitaker's Sport Store
7700 Rome Road
Pulaski, NY 13142
(315) 298-6162

Yankee Fly and Tackle Shop
7541 Salina Street
Pulaski, NY 13142
(315) 298-2466

This is a partial list of services, for complete information
contact:

Oswego County Department of Promotion and Tourism
County Office Building
46 East Bridge Street
Oswego, NY 13126
1-800-248-4386

or

Oswego County Guides Association
PO Box 571
Pulaski, NY 13142

◆